I0560049

ISBN: E-Book # 978-1-968843-08-3

Paperback # 978-1-968843-09-0

Hardcover # 978-1-968843-10-6

Printed in United States of America

Disclaimer: The author and publisher make no representations or warranties with respect to the accuracy or completeness of the contents of this work and specifically disclaim all warranties, including without limitation warranties of fitness for a particular purpose. No warranty may be created or extended by sales or promotional materials. The advice and strategies contained herein may not be suitable for every situation. This work is sold with the understanding that the author and publisher are not engaged in rendering legal, accounting, or other professional services. If professional assistance is required, the services of a competent professional person should be sought.

Cover Design by: Authors Hike

Publisher: Authors Hike

For permission requests, please contact: dreed1232@gmail.com

DAVID REED

Table of Contents

Chapter 1

A God Story

Here is the stunning Bridalveil Falls in Yosemite National Park. Whenever I see the splendors of God's creation, it continues to leave me in awe. I captured this photo during the summer of 2005, a prosperous year for my real estate business, which allowed us to explore the breathtaking sights of the West that we had long dreamed of visiting. Little did I know at the time that this image, and further ones, would one day find a place in a book titled My God Stories," BUT GOD DID.

You will listen to this phrase often throughout this book, designed to emphasize the fact that God is always with us.

This is a close-up view of "Brides Veil," a truly breathtaking location filled with natural beauty and a sense of tranquility. Such moments truly feel spiritual, enabling us to bond with nature and ponder its wonders of creation. Whether it's the stunning views, the sounds of nature, or the feeling of peace that envelops you, such experiences can be profoundly moving.

Transitioning from the thunderous roar of the falls to the serene, gentle flow of the nearby stream is truly a remarkable experience. I am immensely grateful for our God and the breathtaking wonders of nature that surround us.

We could not see the thoughts others were having that day as they witnessed these wonders of nature, but we heard a lot of people expressing themselves with, "Oh my God, this is just amazing." Their words were expressing exactly what God intended: appreciation for his greatness. That is the intent of this book. I will share a few of my God stories and the significant impact they have had on my life, and pray that as you identify with them, you will realize you have a few, or maybe a lot of your own.

As I cover stories that impacted my life and try to illustrate for my readers how the spirit of God was strongly felt in each situation, so much so that I could only say "Thank you, Father."

By recognizing your own God stories, you'll realize that God has been with you throughout your journey life.

Proverbs 16:9: "In their hearts, humans plan their course, but the Lord establishes their steps."

Knowing God establishes your steps, enjoy your walk, and talk with Jesus as you share your God stories.

What if I don't believe in God? Will I still appreciate what you call a God story? The answer is a resounding yes. A belief in God is not needed to appreciate a good life story, especially when it is filled with a powerful message to open someone's heart to see God working in other people's lives.

Chapter 2

Watch Out for The Great Divider

Matthew 22:37 Jesus replied: "'Love the Lord your God with all your heart and with all your soul and with all your mind.'[c] 38 This is the first and greatest commandment. 39 And the second is like it: 'Love your neighbor as yourself.'[d] 40 All the Law and the Prophets hang on these two commandments."

Let me give you a warning that Satan will do all he can to make you scoff at any event being associated with God. He knows God's stories are mighty spiritual truths. You might ask why. We must understand that Satan is the father of **HATE**. He hates God and his followers, so his goal as the great divider is to diffuse all truth. Hate is his greatest tool.

Hate can arise from a variety of sources, and its origins are often complex and multifaceted. Here are some common factors that contribute to the development of hate.

Fear and Ignorance: Fear of the unknown or unfamiliar can lead to negative feelings towards people, cultures, or ideas that are different from one's own. Lack of understanding often breeds misconceptions and stereotypes and results in fear and ignorance.

Socialization: Individuals can learn hateful attitudes from family, peers, or society. Cultural norms, media representations, and social environments can all influence how people perceive others.

Personal Experiences: Negative personal experiences, such as trauma or conflict, can lead to generalized feelings of hate towards certain groups or individuals.

Identity and Belonging: People often form their identities in relation to others. In-group vs. out-group dynamics can foster a sense of superiority, leading to animosity towards those who are perceived as outsiders.

Power and Control: Hate can be used as a tool for maintaining power and control over others. Groups or individuals may promote hate to rally support or justify discrimination and violence.

Psychological Factors: Some psychological theories suggest that hate can stem from unresolved emotions, such as anger or frustration, that are projected onto others.

Historical Context: Historical events and societal conflicts can create long-lasting divisions and resentments that manifest hate in subsequent generations.

Understanding the roots of hate is crucial for addressing and mitigating its effects in society. Promoting empathy, education, and open dialogue can help counteract hate and foster understanding.

LOVE OVERCOMES HATE:

The concept of God's love is often seen as a powerful force for overcoming hate in various religious and spiritual traditions. Here are some ways in which God's love can help to counteract hate:

Unconditional Acceptance: Many religious teachings emphasize that God's love is unconditional and inclusive. This can inspire individuals to embrace others, regardless of their differences, fostering a sense of unity and acceptance.

Forgiveness: God's love often includes themes of forgiveness, encouraging individuals to let go of grudges and resentment. This can help break the cycle of hate and promote healing in relationships.

Compassion and Empathy: Understanding God's love can lead to greater compassion and empathy for others. Recognizing that everyone is deserving of love can help individuals see beyond their differences and connect on a human level.

Transformation of the Heart: Many spiritual teachings emphasize the transformative power of love. Experiencing or reflecting on God's love can lead to personal changes in attitude and behavior, reducing feelings of hate and promoting kindness.

Community and Support: Religious communities often emphasize love and support for one another. Being part of a loving community can provide individuals with the strength to overcome hate and work toward reconciliation and understanding.

Moral Guidance: Many faith traditions teach that love is a fundamental principle. This moral guidance encourages individuals to act in ways that promote love rather than hate, influencing their interactions with others.

Hope and Healing: God's love can provide hope and a sense of purpose, helping individuals to heal from past hurts and move forward positively. This optimism can alleviate the despair commonly linked to hate.

Promoting Peace: Many religious teachings advocate for peace and non-violence. Emphasizing love as a core value can inspire individuals and communities to seek peaceful resolutions to conflicts rather than resorting to hate.

By fostering an environment of love, compassion, and understanding, individuals can work towards overcoming hate, both within themselves and in their communities.

A heart filled with love can profoundly influence an individual's perspective and experiences, allowing them to overcome hate and recognize the presence of God in their life more clearly. Here are several ways this transformation can occur:

Shift in Perspective: Love encourages individuals to see the good in others, even those they may initially dislike. This shift in perspective can help eliminate biases and preconceived notions, allowing one to recognize the divine in every person.

Openness to Forgiveness: A compassionate heart tends to forgive more easily, liberating people from the weight of resentment and anger. Forgiveness aligns with many spiritual teachings and opens the door to experiencing God's grace and mercy.

Increased Compassion: Love fosters empathy, enabling individuals to understand and share the feelings of others. This compassion can lead to acts of kindness, which reflect God's love and presence in the world.

Connection with Others: A heart of love promotes connection and community. Engaging with others in meaningful ways can reveal God's work through relationships, shared experiences, and collective support.

Alignment with Spiritual Values: Many religious traditions emphasize love as a core value. By embodying love, individuals align themselves with these teachings, making it easier to see how God is at work in their lives and the lives of others.

Inner Peace: Love cultivates a sense of inner peace, which can create space for spiritual reflection and growth. This peace can help individuals become more attuned to God's presence and guidance.

Active Participation in Goodness: A caring heart motivates people to participate in service and charitable acts, reflecting God's love in action. This active participation can deepen one's faith and awareness of God's work in the world.

Mindfulness and Presence: Love encourages individuals to be present at the moment, appreciating the beauty of life and the divine in everyday experiences. This mindfulness can enhance spiritual awareness and recognition of God's presence.

Transformation Through Love: Experiencing and expressing love can transform individuals, leading them to a deeper understanding of themselves and their relationship with God. This change frequently leads to a deeper appreciation of life and a sharper understanding of divine purpose.

Community and Worship: Engaging in loving communities and worship can reinforce the feeling of God's presence. Shared experiences of love and faith can illuminate the ways God is working in individual and collective lives.

By cultivating a heart of love, individuals can move beyond hate, fostering a deeper connection with others and a clearer understanding of God's presence and work in their lives. This experience frequently results in personal development, healing, and a more profound understanding of purpose, along with inspiring God Stories.

Power of God's Stories: Stories of God's work in the world—whether through scripture, personal testimonies, or historical events—are seen as powerful because they convey truths about love, redemption, and hope. These narratives can inspire and strengthen believers.

Chapter 3

Legend or Not

Speaking of greatness, we have all heard the saying, "He is a legend in his mind." It was very humbling for me to discover that you do not become a Pickleball legend by just wearing a "T" shirt your daughter gave you for Christmas!

Therefore, kindly refrain from being misled by the shirt; I am not an individual who participates in Pickleball legend. I recently validated that fact when I watched a video of myself playing. I was shocked to see that the young, agile player I expected to see had been replaced by an older, slower version of myself that I hardly recognized! That is what I call a sad God story!

I genuinely enjoy playing Pickleball, but especially the opportunity it provides me to share God's love. Now that I've admitted I'm not a Pickleball legend, I'll say that I'm just another player who stands out more for my faith in God than for my skills on the court. Living in The Villages, Florida, the Pickleball capital of America—God grants me many opportunities to meet new players almost every day.

Subsequent to the passing of my wife in July 2020, I found myself experiencing significant emotional distress and encountering difficulties in progressing forward, often preoccupied with memories of the past.

In February 2021, a dear friend invited me to join him at the Pickleball courts. Initially, I hesitated to respond because the name "Pickleball" did not sound cool. At that time, I had no idea what Pickleball was. I even asked if it was like lawn bowling! He laughed and assured me it was nothing like that.

So, on February 16, 2021, my brother in Christ and Pickleball Teacher, Owen Mitchell, invited me to the courts to discover what Pickleball was all about. After 30 minutes of dinking, learning what the kitchen was, and hitting a few serves, my opinion changed. It was a lot more active than what I had imagined. I will always be thankful for Owen's encouragement!

As I started to play, I observed how most of the good players avoided me, or if they did play with me, they hit hard shots at me that I was not ready to return, so I got hit a lot. With the bruises, I made many new friends on the courts, and some of them helped me through my grieving process. Many were just "snowbirds" that would be gone by the end of April. When I started dating, the morning Pickleball gals I played with became my dating coaches, giving me lots of advice.

After four years of participating in the sport and two years of serving as a USA Pickleball Ambassador, I am pleased to express my genuine passion for Pickleball. I am deeply appreciative of the opportunity to engage with the diverse community and forge connections with many wonderful individuals. From my start, did I ever think I would become a Pickleball Ambassador? Never, but God did because he knew I would use it to glorify him.

As I try to make friends with everyone on the courts (part of my role as an ambassador), many have shared the trials they are facing and asked me to pray for them. I usually respond with; would you like to pray right now? They usually say yes. So, I put my hand on their shoulder and prayed with them. I love sharing God's love every day.

When I look back at the end of my day, I am always thankful when I can clearly see God's busy, miracle filled hands at work in my life.

Many times, I have witnessed events where it seemed that God just performed a miracle for me. It could be as simple as Him leading me to a hurting soul I can pray with.

My favorite expression in response that you will hear throughout this book is: "I did not know that was going to happen, but God did." God directs our steps every day, and we need always to be prepared to respond with love.

Years ago, when I was a youth leader, I used to lead a song by Kurt Kaiser entitled "Pass it On." The lyrics went like this:

It only takes a spark to get a fire going,

And soon, all those around can warm up in its glowing;

That's how it is with God's Love,

Once you've experienced it,

You spread the love to everyone,

You want to pass it on.

What a wonderous time is spring,

When all the trees are budding,

The birds begin to sing, the flowers start their blooming;

That's how it is with God's love,

Once you've experienced it.

You want to sing, it's fresh like spring,

You want to pass it on.

I wish for you, my friend.

This happiness that I've found;

You can depend on God,

It matters not where you're bound, GOD!

The Lord of love has come to me,

I want to pass it on.

When we extend even a small amount of love to someone in need, we can ignite a spark that lights a fire in someone's heart.

When I ask people to name some wonders of God's creation, they often mention places like the Grand Canyon, Niagara Falls, Yosemite, Yellowstone, or other stunning natural sites.

I then remind them that they are the most extraordinary wonder of God's creation. We are the pinnacle of His work. When our "spirit" connects with God, even with faith as tiny as a mustard seed, incredible things can happen; we can move mountains. We are capable of providing support to a fatigued individual, fostering a sense of love; and it is widely recognized that love constitutes the most potent force in the universe.

"My God Stories," serves as a reminder from God to my spirit, encouraging me to share my experiences with others, and hopefully, they will help them to recognize how God is at work in their own lives.

If you have never acknowledged a great God story in your life, then stand by, and maybe my stories will jog your awareness of a few in your own life. I pray my God stories will serve to help you see many God stories in your own life.

After you finish this book, I think you will be amazed just how many God stories you may have already experienced, and hopefully that will challenge you to rise and share the delight of your God stories with others. Then you can genuinely say, I did not know that was going to happen, but God did.

Chapter 4

My Boyhood God Story

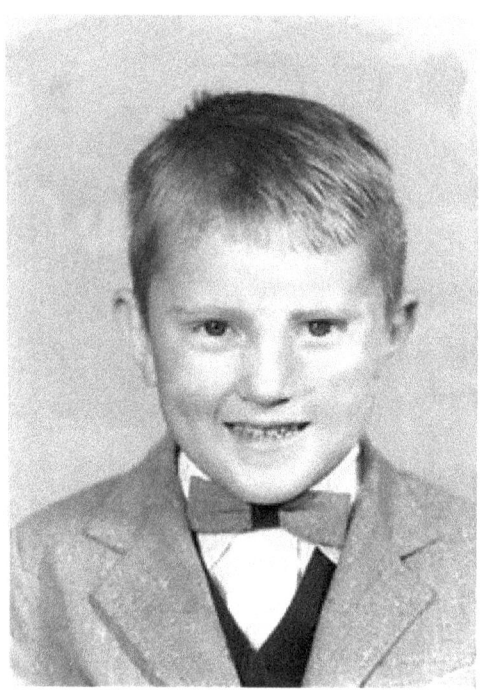

No, that is not my dating photo, it is just the only photo I ever had in a nice suit! Once I outgrew that suit, the next one was on me!! So that took many years. I think this was my college graduation photo; I was a genius!! Ok, I will be straight. It was my first-grade photo! In case you are not aware, that is what cute looks like in the first grade!

Can you see the glaring light of God in those eyes broadcasting a clear message to Satan, "Run, Satan run," a Top Gun for God is born?

I don't want the photo to mislead you, so let me be honest and say that I grew up a poor country boy living in a rural area of Frankfort, Kentucky. My dad was a good guy, but for most of my growing-up years, he was a person with alcohol use disorder, which made life hard for my family. Caring for the family was not my dad's highest priority. At the end of his working week, he would hit the local bars (we referred to that area as "The Bottom"), spend his entire paycheck, and come home broke. Although many times he did not make it home, he would end up in jail for drunk driving and, be there for a few days and lose his job. As a result, there was not enough money to pay rent or feed us, so we struggled to get by another week. If we did not pay the rent, we would have to move, and in my 18 years of living at home, we moved 32 times.

My mother, raised in an orphanage, toiled as a laborer in a factory, earning a modest income. Nevertheless, she succeeded in keeping us nourished with essentials such as tuna, bologna, bread, and Kool-Aid.

My church memories date back to when I was only five years old. My family occasionally attended a small country Baptist church (St. Johns Baptist Church) but was not consistent in attendance, as it depended if my dad had been sobered long enough that he felt ok to attend.

I still remember our first church building on St Johns Road. It was a rectangular wood building with wooden steps leading into the auditorium. It had big, tall windows on both sides that would be raised to get a breeze, as air conditioning was not available in those days. It had an upstairs attic (hot box) where we kids would have our Bible class. There were no windows, just an overhead light so we could see the wasps flying around us. It was a real sweat room!

The adults held their Bible class in the main auditorium. They all had hand fans, and if lucky, a breeze would blow through the open windows.

I was so happy when the church bought a piece of land just a couple of miles up the road and built a basement that fit the budget for a small country church. It was a good upgrade because it had an auditorium, classrooms, and air conditioning.

The brick building in the center was the new facility in those days, but it had a flat concrete roof. They have expanded to include a side building that looks like a children's area and a new air-conditioned auditorium. I did not know I would see this someday, but God did.

When we attended, my mom and a lady named Mrs. Moore taught a Sunday School class for the kids. I can still remember the little one-page Bible Story handouts, our hand fans, and the cookies and Kool-Aide we got each week.

It was during those Bible Classes at a very early age (4-6) that I learned about Jesus and the sacrifice he made for me and the whole world. I was spiritually connecting my young spirit with Jesus. I have sung "Jesus Loves Me" enough times that I believed it in my heart. And yes, I drank the Kool-Aide and ate the cookies, too; that was our reward for being still during the lesson!

I had two older sisters, Dorothy and Barabara. I remember my first youth gathering was to tag along with my older sister Dorothy (Dot) to Red Bridge. I probably rode in the back of the pickup truck so Dot could ride with the young man who invited us to the outing. In those days, a lot of us rode in the back of trucks.

Several of the youth wanted to gather on a Saturday evening at Red Bridge to build a campfire. In those days, Red Bridge was passable. Later in my life when I lived closer, I used to ride my bike down to Red Bridge and dip our feet and sometimes bodies to get cooled down.

However, it was upon the flat rock bed adjacent to the waterfall where we convened, performed musical renditions, roasted marshmallows, and forged a memory that would last a lifetime. I was unaware that this memory would eventually be documented in a publication, though God was aware.

I learned other things as a young boy. I lived in a low-rent country home, which meant we had to learn country survival skills. For our bathroom needs, we had an outhouse (or stink box is what I called it). For running water, we would grab a bucket and dipper and, go to the cistern and draw water by dropping a bucket tied to a rope. Once the water was out of the cistern, we would have to use the dipper in the bucket to get the water bugs out before we took the water into the house.

A lot of things were different in our life. As a country boy, I learned how to shoot a gun and how to hunt when I was six years old.

It was right after the Korean War ended, July 27, 1953, that my cousin, Phillip, came home from the war and spent some time with our family.

He told me I needed to learn how to shoot because someday I might be called to war, and the best shooters win.

In this photo, I am on the back left side, and it was taken just after I returned home from my Air Force Basic Training. I wanted to honor my cousin Philip, the Korean War Veteran, who is standing in the back row between me and my dad. Unfortunately, photos in the 60s were not digital, so it is not a very clear photo.

It had been twelve years since he bought me my first rifle. Others in the photo were my dad on the right, my brother-in-law and nephew on the left, and Philip's red-headed son, who was killed at the early age of sixteen.

In order to adequately prepare me for future military conflicts, he believed it was essential to impart the skills necessary for firearms proficiency. Consequently, he purchased a Remington rifle, specifically a single-shot, bolt-action .22 caliber. Given his military service in the Army, I chose to show my appreciation by affixing an Army decal to the butt of the firearm.

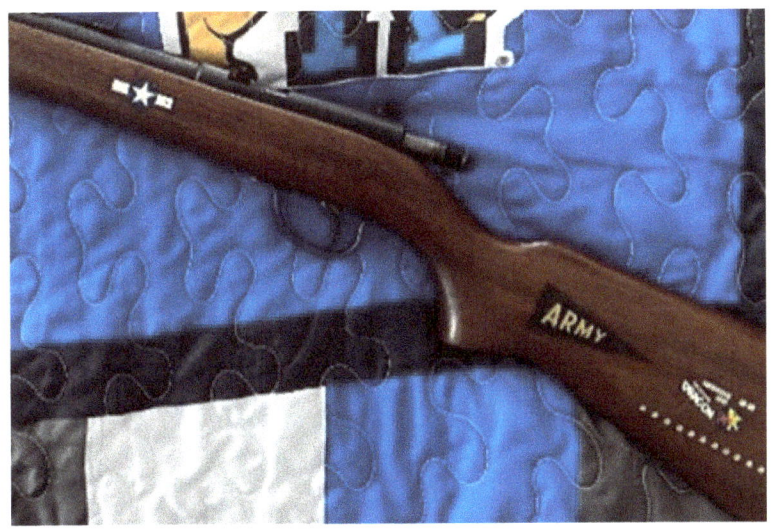

However, for some unknown reason (maybe a future God Story), I was more inclined to like the U.S. Air Force, so I put several Air Force decals on it as well. Keep in mind the Air Force was just created on September 18, 1947 (a year before I was born), so they did not have a lot of aircraft at that time, thus, my decals were limited to the B25 Mitchell and the C47 Flying Dragon.

We did a lot of shooting, and at the mature age of six, I got pretty good at hitting my small tin can and coke bottle targets. Once I established myself to be a good shot, my dad took me to the woods, and I started hunting rabbits and squirrels with my 22 rifles. I'm not bragging, but I was very successful in putting meat on the table!

The image presented above represents a significantly enhanced portrayal of the former residence in which we resided during my cousin's return from Korea. To the left side of the vehicle and down the hillside lay our previous burn pile. It was at this location that I commenced the practice of shooting tin cans and glass bottles, imagining they represented adversaries. I developed considerable proficiency in vanquishing these imagined foes, demonstrating commendable marksmanship skills akin to those of a Top Gun in a rural context.

This is the house in 2024; as you can see, it looks livable now.

My first God story comes from our old house that once sat upon this plot of ground. Unfortunately, that was way before iPhones, so I don't have any photos of our old shack. You will notice the house has a crawl space under it. The house we lived in looked nothing like this.

Our footings around the house were old wooden posts, and open sidewalls to make it easy for all critters to pass through or take cover under our house. We had a tin roof, no siding, and certainly no fresh paint. We even had tins for some of the interior walls.

The crawl space was a great place for snakes to go under the house and find holes in our old wood flooring. Yes, you may have guessed the snakes would occasionally pop their heads through the holes in the floor and sometimes they entered unnoticed and would hide out in our kitchen stove storage drawer. They liked to surprise my dad who hated snakes.

During those days we had a female Cocker Spaniel dog and male Beagle. It was my opinion that the female wasn't too smart. She decided to have her litter of puppies up under the house, where the snakes were.

Being a lover of dogs and fearing the fate of the new puppies, I decided they needed to be rescued. Let me be clear, like my dad, I am very, very afraid of snakes! My mom and dad were at work and my oldest sister was at home but she didn't really keep a close watch on me.

I had been introduced to Jesus and God, so I knew they were very powerful. I had a great fear of snakes, but my spirit led me to pray to God and ask him to protect me. So, I got on my knees, folded my hands, and asked God to watch over me and to keep me safe so I could rescue the puppies. I prayed, and I felt protected. So, with confidence, I entered the crawl space, knowing that God would protect me.

When my dad came home and saw what I had done, he was taken aback. He asked me, "Weren't you afraid the snakes would get you?" I replied, "No, Dad, I prayed for God to protect me before I went under the house." It wasn't until many years later that I recognized this moment as the beginning of my trust in God to shield me from the evils of the world. I wasn't sure if I would encounter a snake or not, but I trusted God, and he protected me then and many more times in my life.

My dad loved to share the story of his young son's faith in prayer and trust in God. I'm not sure if my dad's sharing of my story ever inspired anyone to place their trust in God, but knowing now what I know about God, I believe it likely did.

That moment marked the beginning of my first God story. Looking back, I feel a sense of glory in realizing that my faith was so strong at such an early age. I truly trusted God to protect me.

So, that made me appreciate my mom and Mrs. Moore for being so kind and loving to plant the seed of Jesus in the hearts of the 4 or 5 of us kids that came for the cookies and the Kool-Aid.

James 1:21: *"Therefore, get rid of all moral filth and the evil that is so prevalent and humbly accept the word planted in you, which can save you."*

I always look back and remind myself that I was saved by the word that was "planted" in me. I am very thankful my mother was a planter. I did not know that event would someday be recorded in a book to inspire others to put their trust in God, but God did!

Chapter 5

My First Baptism

Through the early years of my life, we continued to move from the country to the city and back to the country. We attended church very seldom. But we were not forgotten by the church family at St John's. I can still remember that summer day in 1961, when a young Baptist preacher from Georgetown College, working with the St John's Church, came to our home on Taylor Avenue and asked my mom if I would like to go to a Bible Camp that summer.

We had not been to church in a long time, so I was shocked when he came to our house. I am now in Middle School, 7th grade. My mom looked at me and asked if I would like to go, and my answer was an immediate yes.

Keep in mind, that was a very bold commitment for me, I had never been away from home before in my life. So, I was a little apprehensive but excited at the same time. I can still remember the fear I felt when he came and picked me up for the camp. I thought, will I ever come back? I can't remember the young pastor's name, but his friendly, loving nature helped me to relax.

Upon my arrival at the camp and my subsequent interactions with other faith-based individuals, I developed a fondness for the Bible Camp environment. As of today, I am unable to recall the specific location of the camp; however, I do know it was situated in Kentucky, enveloped by trees, featured a murky lake, and was flanked by several mountains. A natural ambiance characterized the setting. We were provided with three nutritious meals daily and were accommodated in cottages equipped with screened windows and ceiling fans. These were the days prior to the prevalence of air conditioning, resulting in considerable perspiration during the day, which led us to eagerly anticipate the cooler evenings. A lot of our daily class sessions were held under shade trees. The camp counselors were all young, energetic, and filled with a very loving spirit.

The guest speaker for the week was a spiritual giant from Miami, Florida. His name was Ted Place. He stood all of 5'3" tall! He joked a lot about his height when he gave his talks, but he was a giant in presenting the word of God. His works were still ongoing in Miami 30 years later when I retired from the Air Force.

My night of commitment came when Ted spoke about surrendering all to Jesus and having our sins forgiven. His words pricked my heart that night; I will never forget that moment. I was so moved by God's word that I went forward to give my life to Jesus. The next morning, I was baptized in that dirty old lake, and my second God story was written. I did not know that with my irregular church attendance that 6 years later would result in me committing my life to Christ, but God did.

Following the baptism, I embarked on a personal journey to ascend the highest mountain available to me. My intention was to draw nearer to God, as I believed that climbing the mountain would facilitate a deeper connection. To this day, I recall vividly the breathtaking view I experienced while seated on the mountainside, overlooking the camp below. In that moment, I engaged in conversation with God regarding my newly cleansed spirit. The experience was profoundly fulfilling; I could have remained in that place for the entirety of my life. However, akin to Moses, I recognized the necessity of descending the mountain in order to fulfill God's calling in my life.

I can still remember being excited and carrying my Bible to school for a while. But like many young people that think they are ready to make that commitment for life, I soon crumbled under the pressure of my peers. God was still deeply in my heart, but I was nowhere close to being a Top Gun for God.

However, on my own, I found a local church in town that I could go to and, so I started attending on my own. I would ride my bicycle to church and back home. That lasted for a few months until one Sunday evening, I was coming home from church, and it was very dark. I had a path across a tennis court, up a little hill, and then down an alley as a shortcut to get home.

Regrettably, on that evening, the lights were inoperative. Typically, the lights would be illuminated due to the frequent use of the courts for outdoor basketball. However, on that occasion, an individual had relocated a dark green metal bench to the base of the hill, precisely at the point where I traversed the courts. The positioning of the metal bench was incongruous, and in the absence of lighting, it was exceedingly difficult to see dark. As usual, I picked up speed, coming across the tennis courts, and then all of a sudden, the bench was there; I crashed, my bike crashed, and I went flying over the handlebars into the metal bench and down to the gravel embankment. I ripped my pants, cut my left leg open, and was bleeding very badly. I still have a 4' scar there today to validate this God story! If my head had hit the bench or the embankment, I could have died that night, but God had other plans for me. I hobbled home (about 300 yards away) crying in pain, but in those days, a hospital visit was out of the question; you just had to heal on your own. As I look back on that incident, I can clearly see Satan was trying to physically stop my persistence in walking close to God.

A few years passed and I was now in High School and not liking it. At the beginning of my junior year, age 16, I hung with older guys who were in college or who had graduated and worked. I wanted to get a job, so I dropped out of High School, took the GED test at Kentucky State University, and passed it. With my diploma in hand, I got a job working for the state as a mail clerk at the Kentucky Health Department. I really enjoyed that job until my boss left, and the lady who took his place was too bossy for me, so I left that job and moved into a sales job.

While concentrating on personal development, I ceased to be a devoted disciple of Jesus. I had not yet acquired the skills necessary to maintain a connection with God while simultaneously engaging in my professional responsibilities. While I knew of God, my spirit wasn't mature enough to surrender my life to Him completely.

My first sales job was an opportunity to work at Adams Shoe store in downtown Frankfort. Mr. Henry Adams was a great man that I really liked and enjoyed learning from. He had stores in several locations throughout the state. He wanted to train me to be a store manager, so after several months he sent me to work for a week at his Bowling Green, hoping I might like it and stay with him and become a manager.

Once I turned 18, I found myself reflecting on my childhood aspirations as I transitioned into adulthood. Over the past few years, the boldness of my faith had begun to fade while my thoughts of joining the Air Force grew stronger. So, I signed up for the delayed enlistment program.

In May of 1967, I received my delayed enlistment call from the Air Force, instructing me to report to Lackland Air Force Base on June 9, 1967.

I dreaded breaking the news to Mr. Adams. I still remember visiting his house to share the news, and both of us felt a sense of sadness. He had been so good to me that I cried as I left his home. But God knew this wasn't the end; I would need his support again in my life. If God could have sat me down and explained all the things He had planned for my life, I would have thought he was describing someone else. I had no clue where he would lead me, but God did.

Chapter 6

Be A Planter

1 Peter 3:15 (New International Version): "But in your hearts revere Christ as Lord. Always be prepared to give an answer to everyone who asks you to give the reason for the hope that you have." But do this with gentleness and respect,

Did you ever sing the song:

"He's got the whole world in His hands".

During my tenure leading youth groups in my earlier years, I recall singing that song frequently, and I consistently appreciated the imagery of God encompassing the entire world within His hands. Reflecting upon my existence as a component of that world, I find myself filled with reverence, contemplating that my presence serves a purpose; He has intentions for my life in each season, from its inception to its conclusion. I just have to be wise enough to seek His path for me.

Matthew 5:16: "In the same way, let your light shine before others, that they may see your good deeds and glorify your Father in heaven."

On April 8, 2024, we experienced God's hands at work when we had a great eclipse from the Southwest part of the US to the Northeast tip of Maine. We watched the moon slowly block out the light of the sun, we call it an eclipse. Or just part of God's wonderful creation since both galactic bodies were created and directed by the powerful hands of God.

Life is filled with spiritual eclipses, but every beautiful sunrise is a reminder that God is with us every morning.

The darkness of sin tries to block out the light of God in our lives every day. Satan is the source of spiritual darkness, and he moves slowly with great deception into our lives to try to block out the light of Jesus.

He starts by getting you to believe a simple little lie. Once he has lured you into his sinful traps, he sets the hook and the spiritual eclipse in your relationship with Jesus begins. As Satan's darkness increases in your life, just like the eclipse, soon, the light of God will grow dim until it is no longer visible in your life.

Truth is not discovered in worldly realms. To assist my readers in perceiving God as He ought to be perceived, I will integrate several expressions of truth extracted from God's Holy Word, the Bible.

Satan has many fooled to believe their worldly source for information is real and so they rationalize their arguments and criticize others with illegitimate information. But as we look at the Love chapter we see the power and the eternal greatness of Love.

I Corinthians 13:8: "Love never fails. But where there are prophecies, they will cease; where there are tongues, they will be stilled; where there is knowledge, it will pass away."

I Corinthians 13:9: "For we know in part and we prophesy in part,"

I Corinthians 13:10: "But when completeness comes, what is in part disappears."

I Corinthians 13:11: "When I was a child, I talked like a child, I thought like a child, I reasoned like a child. When I became a man, I put the ways of childhood behind me."

I Corinthians 13:12: "For now we see only a reflection as in a mirror; then we shall see face to face. Now I know in part; then I shall know fully, even as I am fully known."

From these truths we see that having all the knowledge of this world does us no good, for it will all pass away, but Love NEVER fails, LOVE is eternal, Love is God. Pursue LOVE.

Jesus made clear **John 4:24 (NIV):** "God is spirit, and his worshipers must worship in the Spirit and in truth." Then Jesus said in **John 14:6 (NIV)** Jesus answered, "I am the way and the truth and the life. No one comes to the Father except through me."

He adds to that advice in **John 14:15-17 (NIV)** assuring us that he will give us the spirit of truth; 15 "If you love me, keep my commands. 16 And I will ask the Father, and he will give you another advocate to help you and be with you forever— 17 the Spirit of truth. The world cannot accept him, because it neither sees him nor knows him. But you know him, for he lives with you and will be[c] in you."

God makes clear that he lives in us, and he gives his true followers the spirit of truth, the only truth. So, if we want truth, we need to seek God.

God works in our life and as we mature in the fruits of the spirit. We are able to see our growth and in our lives through our God stories that become clearer to us as we mature.

As a young boy growing up in Kentucky, I vividly remember witnessing God's greatness in the food we cultivated. In the spring, we would use a push plow to till several rows of soil in the fields before planting corn seeds. We would place a seed about an inch deep, cover it, then go down six to twelve inches to drop another seed and cover it as well. After that, we would pray for rain and hope for a bountiful harvest.

It was amazing to watch the seeds sprout through the soil, transforming from tiny seeds into small stalks with little ears of corn. By the end of summer, the fields were filled with tall corn stalks, ready to be harvested, shucked, and eventually cooked for our Sunday lunch.

In those days, a good Sunday meal typically included fried meat, mashed potatoes with gravy, green beans, and corn-on-the-cob. The old folks would scrape the fresh off the cob. On-the-cob, was more fun, as this was before we had corn cob holders! The buttery fingers at the end were quite tasty!

I can still remember how special it felt to eat the corn we had planted.

God asks us to sow his seed of love into the world. We do not create plants or humans, we just plant seeds.

I Corinthians 15:37: "When you sow, you do not plant the body that will be, but just a seed, perhaps of wheat or of something else."

I Corinthians 15:38: "But God gives it a body as he has determined, and to each kind of seed he gives its own body."

As I absorb this message and see so many people every day, I witness God's magnificent creations in those people he created from seeds every day.

God gives us a method to plant the seed for human growth, but He produces the physical body and the plans He has for the spirit he plants in each of us. As disciples we are called to spread the seeds of Christ and love.

The Apostles were reminded of this mission in, **I Corinthians 3:5-7 (NIV):** "What, after all, is Apollos? And what is Paul? Only servants, through whom you came to believe—as the Lord has assigned to each his task. 6 I planted the seed, Apollos watered it, but God has been making it grow. 7 So neither the one who plants nor the one who waters is anything, but only God, who makes things grow."

Like the corn that grew from a seed, or the boy that grew into a 76-year-old man, God never ceases to amaze me how he will plant a seed or a thought in our spirit and then cultivate it, and watch it grow and mature over time into his design and to fulfill His plan that only that special seed of life can complete.

Thats exactly how "My God Stories" came to life? I was in need, God planted a seed, and then He sent me on my way to help it grow and spread His wisdom throughout His Kingdom.

This spiritual wisdom He imparted to me is one of my many personal, God stories! God works in all of us, so we all have God stories. The closer you walk with Him the more you will realize He has protected you and blessed you many times in your life.

This story is preceded by many years of faith and life building challenges. As this seed took root in my soul the vision of its impact upon the world began to grow clearer, as God desired!

The more I contemplated God's hands and his vast purpose, I would see the vision growing, just like the corn stalks in the fields. It soon became clear that God was using my original vision of seeking a way to find a new soulmate to stir my mind in a new way to help other people to grow into a deeper connection with His truths.

As the seed that God planted in my heart began to grow it became clear that the vision had a much bigger purpose by allowing my Top Gun experiences coupled with my God stories to help others to see how He was active in their lives as well.

The personal growth of my faith and trust in God's wisdom have truly been tested through my years of life. Sometimes, I did good and other times I created my own trials.

My God stories are about how God took the trial of losing my soulmate of 49 years and planted a special seed of wisdom related to the many times I could testify that God was clearly walking with me.

He led me to my new wife and she helped encourage me to write my stories. I think this book is God speaking through my spirit with a clear message to share His many miracles in my life so you can begin to see God in your life.

Human beings are not preordained automatons. The Creator has fashioned us for a divine purpose, and from the inception of humanity with Adam and Eve, He bestowed upon us the gift of free will. According to the Scriptures, we are assured that we receive universal assistance from the Almighty whenever we invoke His name.

I was calling upon His name when my first wife passed, and I wanted direction for my life in my pursuit of a new wife.

As we read in the book of Psalms, **Psalms 23**, God says that, "..even though I walk through the valley of the shadow of death, I will fear no evil, for thou art with me.." Knowing that He was with me, and that I needed a soulmate to make me whole, God sent me a clear message on how to start my search for a new soulmate, which became another God story in my life, my first book, Hands of Love. I never thought I would publish a book, but God did.

Chapter 7

Off We Go

As I stated earlier, I moved a lot. One of the places I lived in the sixties, my high school days, was an all-black neighborhood at the end of Logan Street close to the Kentucky River. This was the duplex I lived in. We lived on the left side. All the houses from this corner down to the river are all gone. I can't say for certain, but they were probably taken out by the spring floods that plagued the low-lying areas.

Walter Cleveland, one of my classmates and a dear friend from my high school, lived across the street from me. We would walk to school together and have good chats as any friends would do. We would talk about the craziness of racial discrimination that neither of us liked. We would just say that we wished the world could be more like us and just love one another.

We played football together and ran track together. Let me say Walter was an outstanding athlete. He held the state record for the 100-yard dash for a long time, 9.9 seconds. I think he held records in a few other events. I loved watching him run on the track. He had a beautiful stride. It was more exciting to watch him on an open-field run in football, and no one could catch him. He was awesome!

I went back to that neighborhood in the early 2000s to look up Walter, to share some love, and to talk about old times. I was sad to discover he had passed. But I thanked God for my memories of Walter Cleveland and his big, beautiful, friendly smile and the special moments we had on those walks to school together.

Knowing Walter Cleveland was a great God story of my life. God allowed our spirits to connect and express love for each other and rise above the wrongs of the times. There will always be wrongs in the world, but God and His Love always rise above. Walter and I both shared that love, and it was beautiful. If you have experienced that in your life, then you, too, have a great God story to share.

By the time I was 18, my faith was weak, and that was not good because I was just about to spread my wings and leave home for good and join the United States Air Force.

We are told by Jesus in **Matthew 6:33:** "But seek first his kingdom and his righteousness, and all these things will be given to you as well."

God does not say to us, give me a list of all the things you want. Instead, his message implies that if we seek Him, that is, to have a strong spiritual bond with him, then He will provide the guidance we need to be successful in our walk down the pathway of life and to heaven.

That is not the same as someone who seeks him for earthly pleasures. I really did not know how or what to pray for at that time, and I just knew this was the moment I would leave and never return. It was exciting and scary all at the same time.

I still remember the night before I left, like yesterday, June 8th, 1967. I was 18 years old, lying in my bed and, for the last night, listening to the big homemade box fan my dad had built that was sitting in the window next to my bed. It had a 2x12 board frame, chicken wire across the front, fan blades from an old car, and I think the electric motor was from some old appliance. The fan had a very loud roar that sounded like an airplane engine when it was running. It was so loud you could pray and barely hear yourself talk. But it was powerful and sucked a lot of cool night air into our little country home!

 The next day, I was leaving to enter the United States Air Force. I was excited and, at the same time, a little bit fearful of not knowing where I was going, where my life would end up, or if I would end up losing my life fighting for my country. This was during the peak of the Vietnam War. I was leaving home forever, so I must admit, I was a bit frightened about everything that was about to happen in my life. I thought about the Air Force decals on my rifle and wondered if this was God's plan for my life being fulfilled from when I was 5 years old.

God had answered one of my prayers as my dad had quit drinking, and for my last two years of living at home, he had been attending church. That gave me comfort for my mom.

So that night, I just said a short prayer and asked God to please be with me as I started this journey. I had dreams of someday having a family and taking them to church and being a good husband and father. So, in my prayer, I asked God to please be with my mom and dad that they will be OK and to guide me while on this new journey of life to someday find a good wife that will love Him first, me second, and one that would have a loving desire to be a good wife and mother for the family I hoped to have someday. According to **Ephesians 5:31:** "For this reason, a man will leave his father and mother and be united to his wife, and the two will become one flesh."

With many uncertainties in my path, tomorrow, I will take the first step of that verse and leave home! I never imagined it would really happen, but God did. Remember the rifle decals, that was God writing my life book right before my own eyes. God knew exactly how my life would look at this season of my life. But, at the mature age of 76, I still have that rifle with those decals on it to remind me that God has always gone before me.

The next day, for the first time, I heard real airplane engines (and they made my fan sound like a whisper) as I boarded my first airplane ever and headed to Lackland Air Force Base in San Antonio, Texas, for eight weeks of Basic Military Training.

This was the first airplane I saw when I arrived at Lackland. It was exciting to see what a decal on the butt of my rifle was now right before me. It hit me: I was an Airman in the United States Air Force Air Force.

This was my new home. Notice the windows on the sides of the building; that was our only ventilation in the building, no air conditioning, no fans, just an occasional breeze in the hot summer months in Texas, if we were lucky.

The days ahead were extremely hot, and the nights provided little relief as we slept in those beautiful open-bay barracks without air conditioning.

I still remember the "Brain Washing" class! Our Drill and Academic instructors both came into our classroom with very sad looks on their faces and told us that everyone in our Flight (about 40 trainees) had been selected to go straight to Vietnam from Basic Training. Our hearts sank as we had no technical training and zero battle skills at this point. We were all thinking the same thing: we were going to die! We were so relieved to learn that it was not real; it was just a good demonstration of how brainwashing can deeply impact one's emotions.

The photo above is what an Air Force Airman looks like when he has just graduated from Basic Military Training, enduring the hot summer, scorching heat (June-August) in San Antonio, Texas. I am sure our Drill Instructor made money on these photos, as these photos were staged at his friend's photoshop. None of us got a flight jacket or a cool scarf like that, but we did not care; we looked cool!

After completing Basic Training and starting my Air Force career, I was still very confused about my future. For my first three years, I wandered through life; like a lot of young guys who just left home, and I was a disobedient child of God.

My first assignment was at Wurtsmith AFB, Oscoda, Michigan. Wurtsmith was located on Michigan's east coast on Lake Huron. It was a Strategic Air Command base with B-52 Bombers on active standby and KC-135 Tankers to support the B-52's long-range and long hours of flying time. The Bombers stayed in the air 24 hours a day, seven days a week.

The pilots had a place on the flight line they called the mole hole. They would stay there on a 24-hour alert for one week. In the event of a war they would run to their jets and take off on a mission that only they knew. I volunteered to go there and serve them and their families on

Christmas day (my birthday) and I did not know the pleasure that would give me, but God did.

I worked on the Strategic Air Command (SAC) Switchboard in the building on the left side of this photo. My barracks, before it was demolished, was across the street where the FedEx truck was parked. When the winter chill factors dropped to -50 degrees, it was still a very dreaded cold walk to work.

This was a time when many college graduates were joining the Air Force to avoid being drafted into the Army. Several of my peers that was new to the field of Telecommunications were college graduates. We all had to go through training to achieve a passing score on our skill level test to advance in our field.

At that point, I still carried an inferiority complex, thinking I was not very smart. However, as we completed our training and took our end-of-course test, I was the only one to score in the top 95% percentile. I received a special certificate from our Wing Commander, which was a really strong signal for me. It told me that maybe I could advance my education at some point. Just maybe there was hope for me.

My fellow Airman, Al Koeneke, was a graduate of the University of Kansas. He became my encourager. When he learned that I just had a GED, he reminded me that I did better than him on our Specialty Test. So, in the Spring of 1968, I enrolled in an English course. After two meetings, I was too intimidated and dropped out. It seemed that college was not for me. Little did I know what God had planned for me. He knew that 10 years later, I would get my degree and become an Officer. That was too high of a mountain to climb in my mind. But God had plans for me that I could not even imagine. That is a God story I hope all can grasp. God's planning of my life and yours is far beyond what we can ever imagine.

Years later, in one of my Education Classes, I learned about the Law of Readiness. When someone is ready and wants to know the information, they will grasp it. When someone is forced to learn something they don't have an interest in, it is like pouring water on a rock and expecting it to be absorbed. But when they desire the information then it is like pouring water on a sponge. It is absorbed and stays with them.

After one winter at Wurtsmith, the weather was so cold there (wind chill -56 below zero) that several of us volunteered for Vietnam just to get out of Michigan.

However, in January of 1968, North Korea was becoming more threatening to the South as they had captured one of our spy US, spy boats, the U.S.S Pueblo. So, there was a huge buildup of troops to South Korea for which I got assigned to Osan Air Base.

I arrived there in June 1968, and then on April 15, 1969, they shot down an EC-121 reconnaissance plane. There was great potential for a second war to start up as we were heavily engaged in Vietnam during that time.

That is why our war planners developed a strategic plan for our defense department to be prepared to fight 2.5 wars at the same time. I would say our forces have fallen way short of that posture today.

My living conditions in Korea were quite different from what I had at Wurtsmith. I went from two men to a room to a 16-men open bay barracks.

The cool guy in white holding the cold mug of brew was me, as I was the Captain of our Football team, and we had just finished a game. My Tennessee buddy, Bruce (bottom left) and I stayed in contact with each other up until his passing a few years ago.

We had a day trip to Seoul and enjoyed seeing more of the country we were there to protect.

A lot happened during my time in Korea. I enjoyed the sweet nature of the Korean people. I did not know that someday, 36 years later, I would have the pleasure of hosting a Korean family in my home. It turned out to be this young girl was a future LPGA player, 2016 Gold Medal Winner, LPGA Hall of Fame player, InBee Park.

I was proud that when I met InBee as a young girl and, later, her husband, Nam Ki-hyeop, I could say Hello in Korean. It helped us connect. I could never in my lifetime have projected for that to happen, but God did.

I did not know that I would come back to Korea 10 years later with a college degree and be an Air Force Officer and an Air Weapons Controller, Command and Control Specialist, briefing all the US and Allied Nations ranking Generals in the Pacific on the AWACS interface to the 1979 Team Spirit Exercise, but God did.

After 13 months in Korea, my tour was up, and it was time to relocate. I had an assignment to England but someone switched it and sent me to Alaska, another cold climate.

I transferred to Wildwood Air Station, Alaska (another cold assignment). However, I was not supposed to be reassigned from one remote base to another, so I was offered a reassignment to my base of choice. I chose Lockbourne Air Force Base, Columbus, Ohio, to be close to my home if I decided to get out after my 4 years were up.

It took five months before my assignment was available, but I stayed for an extra month so I could get credit for a second remote.

I did not know that once I became an Officer, I could only have two remotes in 20 years. I did not know that I was going to become an Officer, but God did. God knew I would not want to be away from my family that would not come together for another six years. God's future plans for my life were far greater than I could have imagined.

Chapter 8

Drawing Near to God

Looking back on my life, this is where I can see that God clearly started guiding my thoughts, even though I was not the Christian I knew in my heart I needed to be. Up to this time, I did a lot of drinking and partying, but I went through a stage of deep thought and meditation in Alaska and started asking myself if this was how I wanted my life to go. Did I want to repeat the history of my dad?

As I tried to be honest with myself, I concluded I did not really enjoy this lifestyle. I was transferred to Lockbourne AFB in Columbus, Ohio, in May of 1970. This was the beginning of God's spirit speaking to mine which was the door opener for a very important future God story.

I started playing golf at Lockbourne, and little did I know that I would someday be a golf coach for a Christian School in Mount Dora, Florida. I also coached our squadron flag football team, and that did not end well, as I got a broken ankle and was in a cast for 6 weeks.

During my days of inactivity my soul was searching for peace, and I decided now is the time to make a change. In September of 1970, my spirit called me to draw near to God.

I felt a calling to go to church, and on a Wednesday night, with one of my buddies, Ed Valentine, I asked if I could join him, and he said yes. We were in the same Squadron, and he lived down the hall from me in our barracks at Lockbourne Air Force Base. Ed was a regular attender at the local Williams Road Church of Christ. On that Wednesday night I asked if I could go with him, and he said yes. Little did I know what God had planned for me from that point forward.

It was a Wednesday night Bible study, and the Preacher, Ray Humphries, taught a lesson from **Romans 8:1-8**. The message dealt with our choices to live by the Spirit or by the flesh. It was no coincidence that God wanted me to hear this message. I had been living in the ways of the flesh.

Romans 8:1: "Therefore, there is now no condemnation for those who are in Christ Jesus."

Romans 8:2: "Because through Christ Jesus the law of the Spirit who gives life has set you[a] free from the law of sin and death."

Romans 8:3: "For what the law was powerless to do because it was weakened by the flesh, [b] God did by sending his own Son in the likeness of sinful flesh to be a sin offering. [c] And so he condemned sin in the flesh."

Romans 8:4: "In order that the righteous requirement of the law might be fully met in us, who do not live according to the flesh but according to the Spirit."

Romans 8:5: "Those who live according to the flesh have their minds set on what the flesh desires; but those who live in accordance with the Spirit have their minds set on what the Spirit desires."

Romans 8:6: "The mind governed by the flesh is death, but the mind governed by the Spirit is life and peace."

Romans 8:7: "The mind governed by the flesh is hostile to God; it does not submit to God's law, nor can it do so."

Romans 8:8: "Those who are in the realm of the flesh cannot please God."

The last three versus pricked my heart and was, life changing for me. It was at that moment that I realized why my life felt so conflicted. My spirit was calling me to draw close to God, but the evil spirit of the flesh was tempting me, or brain washing me, to enjoy the things of the flesh. Like the prodigal son, I decided that night that I wanted my spirit to be in synch with God and the things of the Spirit. So, I committed in my heart to pursue more of God's Word and choose life and peace over sin and death. I felt like my boyhood commitment to God was not complete, it lacked understanding and commitment. Although I thought I was in charge, God was truly directing my spirit to a beautiful path that He clearly had planned for me.

Proverbs 16:9: "In their heart's humans plan their course, but the Lord establishes their steps."

I can now clearly say, beyond any shadow of a doubt that God was directing my steps to my future soulmate. It is so beautiful to look back and see that when I started surrendering my spirit to God, He took the lead.

Chapter 9

My Jeannie

In the spring of 1970, I was in Alaska at a remote site in the Kenia peninsula. I had started my transition of not liking the party life and was seeking to draw closer to God. I had no real knowledge of what I really wanted, but my spirit was directing me away from the party scene, and unknown to me, God was directing my path to Ohio.

In May of 1970, I was reassigned to Lockbourne AFB in Columbus, Ohio. In that same month, Luana Jean Coon (Jeannie), from Columbus, Ohio, had finished her junior year at Harding University and was now a senior in college that was engaged to a guy from Columbus.

She had known Jeff since her freshman year of college. Jeannie, with wedding plans already made and invitations already written, decided to end her long engagement. She called off the wedding that spring before coming home for summer break.

She told me many times that she got down on her knees in her attic room and prayed for God to bring her a man who would love her and help her get to heaven no matter what happened in her life. Before her passing she reassured me many times that I was the man she prayed for.

She attended church at the Williams Road Church of Christ all summer with her mom. My buddy, Ed Valentine, went to the same church, so he knew her. In early September, she went back to school for her final year at Harding University in Searcy, Arkansas.

It was late September, and I started attending the same church. You might ask, if God was directing your steps, why didn't He direct you there in June or July? Looking back on the condition of my spirit, the answer is very clear. He wanted me to get my spirit right with Him before he allowed me to meet Jeannie, my future wife.

Unbeknown to me, after attending for a while, Jeannie's mom had written to her and told her that there was a good-looking young guy from the Air Base attending their church. Jeannie told her mom that she was not interested in dating any military men.

But the Spirit was communicating to her mom because her mom told me she knew from the moment she met me that I was the one for Jeannie. Keep in mind, at that time, I barely knew her mom and I still did not know Jeannie even existed. Are you feeling the movement of the Spirit?

Ok, I know she is beautiful, but quit looking at her picture and get back to the story.

Just two months later, in November, on a Wednesday night, God began to reveal His plan for me. He brought a beautiful girl to that small church in Columbus, Ohio. She was home on Thanksgiving break from her senior year at Harding. She had a special glow about her, and I was immediately attracted to her. I felt like the angels were singing, and the bells were ringing all around her as she lit up the auditorium with her presence.

I did not know this was going to be the biggest life-changing moment of my life, but God did. I did not know that night we would fall in love and get married, but God did. I did not know I would be taking her home that night after the youth gathering at the Thompson house. I had never heard of the game of "spoons" until that night. But I saw that beautiful, spirited young woman enjoying the fun of the game, and I was thrilled that she sat at the opposite end of the table from me, allowing me to admire her all evening. I loved having her beside me in my car as I drove her home after the event. I was overjoyed when she answered my call the next day and accepted my invitation for our first official date on Friday night.

I appreciated her flexibility when I drove up to the Fair Grounds for a car show, only to discover there were no cars around and that the event was actually scheduled for two weeks later. I loved that she was content to simply share a pizza and talk for hours. I still remember the happiness I felt just being with her.

God spoke to me clearly that night as He revealed to me that this precious soul was going to need someone to protect her, love her, and help lead her to heaven. I did not tell her, but I accepted that role before we finished our pizza that night, but my strategy to get her there was not in place, just yet.

My buddy Ed had known her as he had been attending the same church during her summer break before I started attending. So, after Ed introduced me to Jeannie, he never let me forget that I owe him big time! But we both knew it was God that directed my steps.

I just want to say a few kind words for my dear friend and Christian Brother Ed, who passed around the same time Jeannie did. God allowed our paths to cross several more times before he passed.

After his retirement he developed his art skills and painted a picture of Amen Corner at Augusta National Golf Course, just for me. For his family's sake, I wanted to honor Ed and post a copy of that painting that still hangs in my living room.

Rest in Peace, Brother, and I will see you soon!

God's hand was truly at work, and I did not even know it. It is so amazing to look back on my life and see all the things God did to bring us together. God worked miracles in both of our lives to connect our paths. He had the future of David and Jeannie Reed all planned out, but we didn't have a clue. All my friends would ask me, how in the world did you get such a beautiful woman? I would just say God did it, and that was my best God story that I got to live for almost 50 years.

We met at church on a Wednesday night, we fell in love, got engaged on our third date, and 8 months later, we were married. Our engagement was so unreal that it humored both of us for the rest of our lives, so I must share this "Only God Knew" story with you.

We met several times at church during her Thanksgiving break and then later during her Christmas break, but we only had two official planned dates. As I previously stated, that date did not go as planned, but it was still a great date. I still remember thinking at the end of our pizza night that she really needed to have an experienced guy like me to protect her. She was a precious soul.

I saw her again at church on Sunday and offered to drive her to catch her ride back to Harding. Her rendezvous point was about 30 minutes south of Columbus. I was so glad to be able to spend a little more time with her as I drove her to Washington Courthouse, Ohio, to catch her ride back to Harding on Sunday afternoon (my first Uber duties).

However, my heart sank as she pulled away; I still did not know what God had planned for us. I just knew in my heart I wanted to be with her, and she was going the opposite way.

I really liked her, but thinking in the back of my mind that she has one semester left of college, and I am sure one of those senior classmen will be pursuing her hard before they graduate. At that time, I had no college, so I felt a bit inferior to even thinking about dating her. To me, just having a GED made college a giant hurdle that could keep us from coming together.

I can still remember thinking that she was headed south on a long 14-hour ride back to Harding, where there would be many guys looking to connect with her before they graduated in the spring. I wanted to go with her, but I still had six months left in my 4-year commitment before my time was up. Little did I know that the Air Force had early out programs for those who wanted to pursue their education.

After she got back to Harding, I just had to give her a call to see if she had any interest. So, I called her dorm, but the girl that answered said she was at the library. Being the persistent guy that I am, I called the library, and she came to the phone and was surprised that it was me. She was thinking it was her mom, and someone had died!

Getting calls in the library was quite rare! We talked just briefly but I told her that I really enjoyed our time together and asked if she would like to go out again when she came home for Christmas, and she said yes. I was a very happy Airman as I floated down the hallway to my buddy Ed's room to share my good news!

I was attending a special Bible study with one of the Deacons, Dick Thompson, and when she came home for Christmas, I invited her to go to the study with me.

I was certainly attracted to her but was not really sure if it was mutual just yet! As we studied God's word together, we clearly connected spiritually. Jeannie's faith was a little more mature than mine as she had been attending a Christian University for the past four years and had sat at the feet of some great men of God.

That's me kneeling and Jeannie in the yellow and black dress

56

But that Sunday night, December 20, 1970, at the end of my class, I decided to get Baptized. Jeannie and the Thompson family went to the church building and, witnessed my baptism, and welcomed me into the family of God. It was really a special moment for me.

When I came out of the water, I felt the Holy Spirit ascend upon me. I felt a strong calling to teach the good news of Jesus. It was very real, and I have continued to do so for the past 55 years. From my first lesson in Romans 8, through my follow-on classes, and now my baptism, I was truly transformed and committed to living a life to serve and honor God. I had no idea this was going to happen, but God did.

I was very excited to go to church on Wednesday night, December 23, and share my good news with all the other members of the congregation. My birthday was Christmas day, and that was just two days away, but this one felt special because I had just received the greatest gift of my life, the gift of the Holy Spirit.

After church on Wednesday evening Jeannie invited me to another family's house after church for a social fellowship. Much to my surprise, Jeannie had planned a surprise birthday party for me. As a new member of this church family, I was very surprised and humbled at the same time. I was certainly getting a strong hint that this very beautiful senior in college, a Christian girl, might be taking a liking to me!!!

After the party, I decided I would go to my hometown, Frankfort, Kentucky, on Saturday, December 26th, to share my good news with my parents. It was about three hours away. I asked Jeannie if she would like to go with me, and she said yes. I thought that her desire to go with me was another very positive sign that we were connecting spiritually.

(The house on the right is where I lived when I took Jeannie to my home.)

We completed our visit with my parents, toured the capital building in Frankfort, and then headed back to Columbus. I drove to Georgetown, where we connected with I-75 North, got a cup of coffee, and stopped at a roadside rest to drink my coffee before getting on the busy I75 interstate. It had been a "really beautiful" winter December day, with clear blue skies and temps in the mid-50s.

As we were sitting there in my cool 1966 Blue Chevrolet Malibu, I said to Jeannie, it sure was a BEAUTIFUL day, wasn't it? She replied, yes, it was. I asked, don't you wish all your days could be as BEAUTIFUL as this? She shocked me when she responded and said, is that a proposal? Wow, this old Kentucky Boy had to think quickly on his feet, but I took a big chance and said YES! I looked at her, and she said YES!

This photo was taken by Jeannie's mom when we told her we were engaged.

Just like that, we were engaged, and I don't think I had even told her that I loved her yet!!! I guess her spirit, and mine were communicating love through the invisible nature of the Spirit, and God was directing our paths. So, just like the miracle of Mary being impregnated through the spirit, God's plan was bringing us together. Some folks said we moved too fast, but it lasted to her end, almost 50 years!

I did express my love to Jeannie in a big way as I applied for the Air Force College Early Out Program and was approved and able to get out in time to attend my first year of college with Jeannie as she finished her last semester at Harding University.

I applied for acceptance at Harding and got in on probation, since I only had a GED. In early January I was released from the Air Force and happily drove my wife "to be" back to Harding. I was excited to be with Jeannie but sacred in my boots to go to college as I had never developed good study habits. Once I got on the campus and got started my confidence gained daily just being with Jeannie and meeting all of her friends. I felt so honored to be with her for her last semester at Harding. The BIG PLUS was I got to date her every day for the rest of her life.

We went back a few years later to capture a front-facing photo in one of Harding's Love Swings.

On June 5, 1971, we made it official and got married at the Williams Road Church of Christ, where we met. It was a REALLY BEAUTIFUL day!!!

So, after getting engaged on the third official date, we felt honored that our marriage lasted 49 years, one month and 24 days.

We kept up our pace as fast movers as Jeannie was pregnant with our first child two months after we were married. So yes, we had our first child in April before our first anniversary in June. For sure, we did not know that was going to happen, but God did

Chapter 10

God Takes The Wheel

When we discovered that Jeannie was pregnant after two months of marriage, we decided it was best for me to go back into the Air Force and finish my career. Our first assignment together was at Little Rock Air Force Base in Little Rock, Arkansas. We had our first child there, Luana Jennifer Reed, born on April 19, 1972.

Jeannie was hired to work at Central Arkansas Christian School in North Little Rock. We met several people from our church family that I still hold as dear friends to this day, especially the Horton family.

This photo was the only photo of me with my mom and dad, as my dad passed just a few months after coming to visit us in May 1972. Jenny was just one month old. I did not know that would be the last time to see my dad in good health, but God did, and I was so thankful I got to share my first child with him.

One of my favorite memories at Little Rock was connecting with a couple of our Harding friends, Dana Cowart (a triplet) who taught at the Christian School with Jeannie, and Stacy Sikes, a friend who graduated from Harding the same time as Jeannie. He was now an Airman in the Air Force.

We would meet at our house once a week and, sit on the floor, and have a weekly devotional together. Stacy was a great artist but was far away from his girlfriend in California. Back in the 70s a long-distance phone call was very expensive to make. Stacy made me an offer, he said Dave, if you will let me use your phone to call my girlfriend in California to get engaged, I will give you this painting of the sailboat in rough seas. My response was, get on the phone!

I had seen the painting, and I did not know I would get such a great deal, but God did. Stacy was asking his girlfriend to marry him over the phone. Guess what? I did not know that I would still have that painting hanging on my wall today in 2024, but God did.

Before finishing the book, I tried to locate Stacy and tell him that his painting would be in my book. Unfortunately, he had passed. I hope some of his family members will get word of it being in the book. I know they did not know his artwork would appear out of nowhere and be in a book, but God did.

Shortly after our daughter, Jenny, was born on April 19, 1972, I got a Permanent Change of Duty assignment to Okinawa. So, in June of 1973, I had to leave my young family and start my tour in Okinawa. At that time Okinawa was going through the Reversion of US Control back to Japanese Control, so housing was getting to be more difficult to find for new families arriving.

But I was eager to get my family together, so I moved quickly. My Commander said I was the fastest he had seen to date, as I had my house locked up in less than 30 days. Your family could not travel until you had housing available. Jeannie did not like the new, no A/C, snails climbing the exterior walls, lizards inside the house, and certainly not the high humidity that would fall upon your interior floors at nighttime.

Over the next three years, we accomplished a lot. I committed to go back to school when I drove down a street on Kadena and saw the small houses on the left for enlisted guys and the big houses on the right for the Officers. I wanted to provide better for my family, so I drove to the Education Office and, enrolled with the University of Maryland, and started back to school, attending night classes after work. I had most of my hours for my bachelor's degree completed by the time our three-year tour was completed. Jeannie had the pleasure of teaching in the DODDS system (Department of Defense Dependent Schools), which she loved, and she also delivered our second child, Kimberly Michelle Reed, on August 26, 1974, at Camp Kui Hospital.

Shortly after Kim was born, we moved to Naha Air Base into On Base housing. Prior to that, we had been living off base near Kadena AB, where I worked and went to school at night to seek my undergraduate degree. The drive from Naha to Kadena was about 20 miles. We drove it everyday morning and evening. My next God story occurred on that drive one morning.

The speed limit was 35mph, but the traffic flow was usually around 45mph on this 4-lane road. I was driving, and my wife, Jeannie, was in the passenger seat. We had a stop light coming up, and traffic was blocked in both lanes. I hit my brakes to slow down, and the pedal went to the floor.

Oh NOOO! I told Jeannie to brace herself. The light ahead was red, and both lanes of traffic were blocked. I swerved right to avoid the traffic. I had no idea what I would hit, I just wanted to avoid collision with other vehicles. God knew at that very spot there was a maintenance area with metal horses blocking the lane, but there was also a pile of sand just past the horses. I went right through the horses, hit the sand pile, and came to a hard, fast stop that threw sand forwards and hit a man that had pulled over on the other side to fix a flat tire. The sand did not hurt him, and it just scared him.

My first thought was to check on Jeannie and then to thank God that we survived the crash. When I analyzed all of the factors that saved us, I told Jeannie that God was really with us, and she said amen to that. On the 20-mile stretch, we were at a stop light that was backed up with traffic, and I did not know what I was going to hit when I swerved right, but God did. We were so near death, but that was not God's plan.

The guy fixing his flat drove us to the hospital as my car was stuck in the sand, and Jeannie had a jammed back and sore knees from hitting the under-the-dash A/C unit. I was unharmed. My shoulders were tense as my grip was so tight that I bent my steering wheel on impact. After that incident, I realized that God was, for certain, walking close by my side and protecting me. I thought, what a miracle! My walk with God was greatly STRENGTHENED by this moment.

God would soon reveal to me my real purpose for being in Okinawa. He had seeds that needed to be planted for the future of the island. Our family attended and served in the Ojana Church of Christ with some of the greatest Christian families of my lifetime. I can say without a doubt that God led me to that very special group of Christians that 50 years later remain close with each other.

One special guy was a young Marine who showed up one Sunday, and after the services were over, we invited him to our house for lunch, something we did to any new person attending for the first time. His nature seemed quiet and shy until he saw my guitar. He asked if he could play it. We had several guests from the church there, and we were all kind of shocked as the quiet guy was about to be exposed. When he started playing and singing songs of John Denver, Jim Croce, and others, we all had a jaw-dropping experience. God only knew what that experience would produce. He was invited to our home on a regular basis, and that open-door spiritual connection inspired Frank Summers to go to a preaching school in Texas and become a pastor. I still stay in contact with Frank as he is still one of my favorite guitarists. Frank says that our hospitality meant more to him than we could ever know. We did not know, but God did.

During our Okinawa days, I did a lot of teaching Bible Classes and preaching and had the pleasure of working with the youth and planting the seed for a Bible camp on the northern end of the Island in the small Village of Sosu.

This Sosu Bible Camp idea was truly a God-inspired seed, and I was just the vessel to plant it. This was clearly one of the most important reasons God sent me to Okinawa. I like to always give credit to Brother Uza, a University Professor and Pastor of the Naha Japanese Church of Christ, for leading the way once the seed was planted. We referred to him as the Elder of the Island.

God inspired me through the spirit to ask the Ojana elders what they planned to do with the Sosu property on the north end of the island. They had the property under church ownership for a long time, but it was not being used. Being only in my 20s and working with the youth, I asked the elders if we could build a bible camp. They said we would need to coordinate with Brother Uza, and they suggested I contact him.

I called Brother Uza that night to see if he had time to meet. He invited me and Jeannie to come to his house in Naha Tuesday evening for dinner. We arrived and sat on the floor around a Japanese-style table and enjoyed their hospitality. When I told Brother Uza the purpose of the visit, he said wait here. He walked into the back part of his house and came back with the plans for the first building, including the total costs. It was not very much. I asked him if he could come to church on Wednesday night. He said yes.

After church, we met with the elders, and Brother Uza presented his plans. They all agreed, and within two weeks, we had the funds to start the project. I took my family and the youth there several times to help construct the first building. I left in June and the first camp was in July.

I have heard through the years that many people went to camp there and that even Japanese people from mainland Japan and the Village of Sosu were baptized there. Another seed planted for God was growing and producing fruit. Looking back, I think that was one of my best God stories. The people who attended the first camp and many that followed never knew who planted the seed, but God did.

During my tour in Okinawa, I developed some heart issues and came to live with us in Okinawa. My dad passed away in October 1972. We brought her to live with us, and I was glad she got to be there to meet our great Christian family. As we were nearing the end of our time in Okinawa I attended the NCO Leadership School as part of my leadership development. I graduated from the NCO Leadership

School and again surprised myself with how well I could do by applying my Godly principles to my military training.

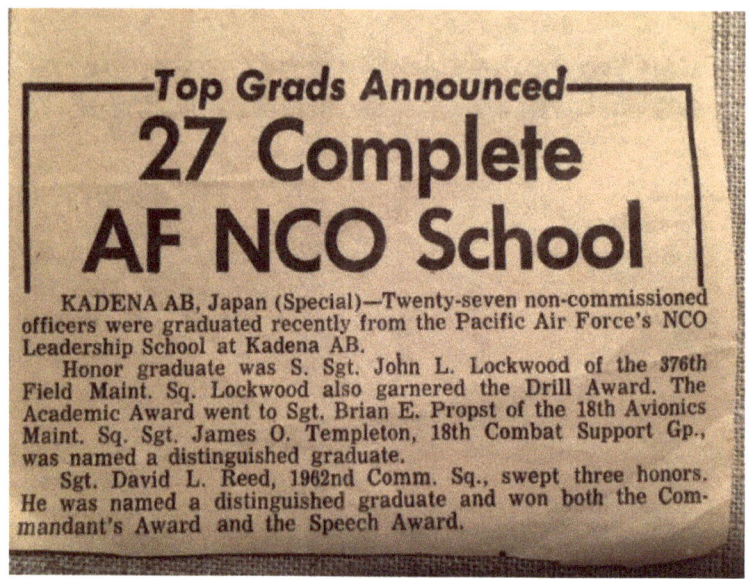

―Top Grads Announced―
27 Complete AF NCO School

KADENA AB, Japan (Special)—Twenty-seven non-commissioned officers were graduated recently from the Pacific Air Force's NCO Leadership School at Kadena AB.

Honor graduate was S. Sgt. John L. Lockwood of the 376th Field Maint. Sq. Lockwood also garnered the Drill Award. The Academic Award went to Sgt. Brian E. Propst of the 18th Avionics Maint. Sq. Sgt. James O. Templeton, 18th Combat Support Gp., was named a distinguished graduate.

Sgt. David L. Reed, 1962nd Comm. Sq., swept three honors. He was named a distinguished graduate and won both the Commandant's Award and the Speech Award.

I was honored that my wife and my mom got to be there for my graduation. I received three awards which were a huge boost to my confidence. I was starting to see that this old High School Dropout, , could accomplish bigger things than I ever imagined. I had no idea that I could achieve such awards, but God knew. He had bigger plans for my life, much bigger. I thought this was my pinnacle, but I am sure God laughed and said, you have only just begun to see my plans for you.

After completing Leadership school and taking three awards, I was asked to join the staff and become an instructor. I really wanted to accept the offer, but my vision led me to Lackland AFB in San Antonio, Texas, which was right next door to the Officers Training School (OTS).

I had prayed that once I completed my degree that, I could apply and hopefully be accepted for OTS. I thought it would be perfect to have my family right there for my graduation. God put that thought into my head because that was exactly where he was leading me: to achieve much greater things.

Chapter 11

A Dream Fulfilled

We arrived at Lackland AFB in San Antonio, Texas, in July 1976. As stated above, I requested this assignment so that when I completed my hours for my BS Degree, I could apply for Officer Training School (OTS), which would be only two miles from my duty station at Lackland. That means my family would be nearby, a real plus when you love your wife and want to keep her close. It worked out perfectly. As I drew closer to the completion of my degree, I applied for OTS and was accepted. Unfortunately, my graduation from college was two days after I had to report to OTS. I got into OTS, but I missed my college graduation.

I also had the pleasure of serving as a Deacon for our youth program for the Lackland Terrace Church of Christ during our time there. While serving as a Deacon, I experienced a huge God moment in my life.

I was offered an opportunity to preach for the congregation on a Sunday night. My message was very simple: it is time to quit procrastinating, get motivated, and do the work God has called us to do. I felt like I communicated the message with great enthusiasm, and the results reflected that it was greatly RECEIVED. About 30 people responded to the invitation. Wow, I did not expect that, but… God did. It was a very rare moment for that church. Usually, if anyone responded to a message, it would only be one or two people. I was so shocked as I was not expecting such a response. One of the Elders came forward and said this must have been what it was like on the day of Pentecost. God knew I needed a confidence and boost, and He knew the lives he wanted to touch that evening. I was so amazed that my simple sermon: Procrastination, Motivation, and Works, would have such an impact. I still have the outline and will look at it on occasion, just to remember that special moment walking down my pathway to heaven. I did not know that would happen, but God did.

Obviously, that was a great spiritual moment, but God had much bigger plans for my life. Looking back on my time there, that was probably my most important spiritual moment of growth, save the birth of our third child, and my only son, Jonathan David Reed, February 3, 1978.

OTS started at the end of May 1978 and was over 90 days later at the end of August. I graduated and left immediately for Eglin Air Force Base. We had received a word that there was Officer housing available for us on base if we could be at Eglin the next morning. So, we drove all night from San Antonio to Ft Walton Beach, Florida, Eglin Air Force Base, and got there in time to get our housing, 32 Bens Lane. I was finally in Officers' Housing! My dream from 1973, driving through the housing area on Kadena Air Base, was being realized in August 1978. I had no idea that the dream would come true. But God did. I was beginning to see that my dreams were not just dreams, they were seeds or visions planted by God.

Psalm 23:

A psalm of David.

1. The LORD is my shepherd, I lack nothing.

2. He makes me lie down in green pastures, he leads me beside quiet waters,

3. He refreshes my soul.

   He guides me along the right paths for his name's sake.

4. Even though I walk through the darkest valley,[a]

   I will fear no evil, for you are with me; your rod and your staff, they comfort me.

5. You prepare a table before me in the presence of my enemies.

   You anoint my head with oil; my cup overflows.

6. Surely your goodness and love will follow me

   all the days of my life, and I will dwell in the house of the LORD forever.

I hope by now you are beginning to see through my God stories that God does guide us down the right paths of life. I am hoping my stories have triggered memories in your life where you can acknowledge God was there for you. Hopefully, you are thinking of someone who will benefit from your stories. Go tell them as soon as you are done with this book.

Chapter 12

Top Gun School

I spent two years at Eglin Air Force Base, developing my skills into one of the best Air Weapons Controllers in my Squadron. Many of the pilots I controlled became good friends, and most just remembered me by my Tactical Call Sign, "Shadow"! Because of my success, I was selected to attend the Aggressor, Red Forces, Top Gun Program, called Fighter Weapons School. It was a three-month program held at Nellis Air Force base in Las Vegas, Nevada. We were trained in Enemy Tactics that we would fly against the Blue Forces to train them how to recognize and defeat the enemy. After graduation, I was assigned to Clark Air Base, Philippines, 26th Aggressor Squadron.

Looking back at that young 6-year-old boy from the hills of Kentucky, who entered the Air Force in the bottom one percent with a GED, I could never have imagined that God could take me from the bottom one percent in the Air Force to eventually the top one percent of all Air Force Officers. Being selected to attend the Top Gun School, meant I had achieved the top one percent in my field. I know you are probably thinking that was truly a miracle!! Me too! But God didn't.

My post-school assignment was to Clark Air Base in the Philippines, 26th Aggressor Squadron, the Best assignment of my career. We traveled all over the Pacific Theatre training U.S. Forces and our Allied Nations (Japan, Korea, Malaysia, Indonesia, Taiwan, Thailand, Australia, New Zealand, Brunei, Philippines) on how to defeat the enemy threats within that operating theatre. I had the pleasure of training a lot of the weapon controllers of many countries and eating a lot of crazy foods, but pigeon heads were the worst. I was honored to have served with a lot of great guys, Blue and Red Forces, that became future Air Force leaders: Conan, John Corley, Commander of the Air Combat Command, Mark Polansky, Jeteye/Roman, and an F-15 pilot from Kadena AB, Okinawa, Kevin Chilton, "Chili," moved on to become Space Shuttle Commanders, and Chili returned to the Air Force and became a four star General and the Commander of the Space Command.

During my time serving in the Aggressor Squadron, I was selected to lead the 1982 William Tell, Air Weapons Control Team, for the 18th Tactical Fighter Wing, to compete in the International Air to Air Weapons Meet, at Tyndall Air Force Base.

This is a competition where all of our US Forces, Canadian, European, German and other Allied Nations come to compete to see who is the best in the World. Through our team efforts and hard training, we won the Competition and were the first team ever to kill all 12 Targets in Profile 4, which was 4 Fighters vs 12 Targets in Profile.

For a poor Kentucky boy who started with just a GED upon entering the Air Force, I was feeling pretty accomplished to now be in the Top 1% of all the men and women in my field.

But even when I was at what I thought was the peak of my career, God had even greater things planned for me. When you walk close to God, he can lead you to greatness, which in turn creates many God stories to share for the encouragement of others.

I had ONE bad day in golf and Jeannie won!!!

I had learned to see God in my life and give all credit for my accomplishments to Him, He was directing my steps. I had learned that a disciplined life was critical for success, especially in my walk with God. When we start each day, we decide if we will start with God or go it alone. Since God is love, it is impossible to please God if you are not plugged into his love. You also will never see his works in your life if you are not plugged into his love.

When I consider my roots, I never had any dreams of being so privileged to walk down such an exciting path in life. I never thought of myself as a high achiever. I was just David Reed, the country boy, but God said I can do wonders through you if you just follow me. So, it is truly a great God story to see this country boy go from the bottom 1% as an Airman to the top 1% in his field in the U.S. Air Force.

I connected well with the hand verse in **Deuteronomy 2:7**, where God reminded Moses that He had been with him for 40 years. It made clear to me that the same God had been carrying me in His hands all of my life. One big God story!

We may think we make our own successes in life, but God clearly says, I got you! He has led me to places I could never have imagined in my lifetime.

At this point in my life, I thought I had achieved all that I could ever achieve. I felt I had reached the pinnacle of my life, but God probably laughed and said, if you could only see what I have planned for you. I did not know, but God did.

Chapter 13

Beyond My Aggressor Days

My career transitioned to Sumter, South Carolina, Shaw AFB, to the 507 Tactical Air Control Wing. This was the largest Wing in the U S Air Force. I believe we had 26 Air Force Units spread throughout 13 states. Our Wing was a Mobile Command and Control System that included a vast array of technology and flying assets. It was referred to as the Tactical Air Control System. Everyone was trained to be combat-ready. We had to be prepared to respond to any wartime activity within 24 hours.

During my time there, I experienced three more giant steps in my career and my life.

The first one came when I was trying to source a Team Leader for a special mission to Honduras, which could last up to six months. The mission was to lead a Mobile Training Team to Set Up a Command-and-Control System for the Honduran Air Force. It was a time when there was a lot of turmoil in the region, and that kept many from volunteering for the mission. After searching for weeks to find someone and coming up empty-handed, I volunteered to accept the leadership role for the mission.

After developing a very ambitious program, I set out to assemble the rest of my team. By the end of March, I had my team of five put together, and we began writing our plan for the mission. The plan was approved, and we were off to get started in April of 1986.

Our mission was to set up a Command-and-Control System by training the pilots and controllers on how to work together to detect and destroy hostile threats. The four members of my team would stay at the base in Tegucigalpa and train radar technicians on how to communicate and plot enemy aircraft detected. I would take two officers on a one-hour drive through some dangerous routes to the mountaintop where the new ANTPS-70 radar had just been installed. My role was to train Honduran Air Force officers on how to control their fighter aircraft to detect and destroy enemy threats. At that time, the biggest threats were the drug missions coming out of Colombia, flying across Nicaragua and Honduras on their way to deliver drugs to Mexico.

Near the end of my mission, we were able to detect and shoot down a drug plane carrying over 200 million dollars' worth of cocaine. This was a great success for our program. It was **My First BIG achievement since leaving what I thought was the highlight of my career**! Before we drove back to the base from our mountain top location, the news had gone from the President of Honduras straight to President Ronald Reagan, declaring a great achievement.

When we walked into the Officers' club, the Commanding General of the Honduran Air Force was there. As soon as he saw me, he called me to the middle of the room where he stood boldly celebrating our success. He handed me a glass of whiskey and challenged me to drink it down in celebration of our great day. Let me be clear, even though I am from Kentucky, I don't drink whiskey, but I had to make the American Fighting Soldiers proud, so I gulped it all down and got a great cheer from everyone in the club. It was a historical moment for the United States and Honduras.

The next week, Vice President Bush came down to meet with the President of Honduras.

For the great success of our team, the Commanding General for the Honduran Air Force informed our Air Force leaders that this was the best team he had ever had in his country. That was a real feather in my cap.

That noteworthy achievement and comments were documented in my Officer Evaluation Report (OER). My OER was sent to the Tactical Air Command Commander, Four-Star General, General Robert D. Russ, to be signed and marked for a Below-the-Zone promotion to Major. Guess what, he signed it, and it happened, I was promoted below the zone to Major (**My second Big Event**), and that put me in the top 1% of ALL Air Force Officers, in the U S Air Force. I would have NEVER imagined that happening to me, a country boy with a GED. But God did.

From that promotion, I was offered a command job in the 71st tactical air control squadron, MacDill AFB, Tampa, Florida, or a job in the legislative liaison office at the Pentagon. I chose to take the Command Job.

I helped elevate my Squadron's rating from a Marginal rating in February to an Operational Readiness Inspection Rating of Excellent in August (**My Third Big Event**). Only the top officers get selected for a command job, so again I kept pinching myself and saying, "Wow." By now, I know it is God leading me, so I just add, Thank you, Father.

Chapter 14

Losing Jeannie

My family was entering a season of needing me present. I just missed my oldest daughter's High School senior year, my middle daughter was going to be a Junior, and my son was entering Middle School. I felt a stronger pull for my family than I did in my career. I felt it was a critical time for me to be with my family, so I retired on July 31, 1990.

I drove out of the gate of MacDill AFB, and 90 minutes later, I was in Eustis, Florida, my new home for the next 34 years.

I enrolled my two kids into a Christian School, Mount Dora Bible School, later named Mount Dora Christian Academy. My wife had always wanted to teach in a Christian school, and so she got her wish, and our roles changed. God began blessing Jeannie more than she could ever imagine.

She did not know she would grow to be the most loved teacher in her school, and a famous golf coach, but God did.

Looking back over our lives, we know for sure that God had purposefully directed our paths together to accomplish His plan for our lives. We raised three kids who are all Christians, and together we enjoyed knowing and loving five grandchildren who are also all Christians.

Through all our years together, our home was known for being a house of hospitality and provided a connection to God's Family for many people in their walk with Christ.

In our latter years, we coached and played golf together and led many Bible classes in our home. Our house was known as the house of love and hospitality. Then, after 49 wonderful years of life as Christian soulmates, God called her home. I kept these photos on my office counter for one year before I began to move forward with my life.

Right to left, Jeannie's Seasons of Life: High School, College Senior, Marriage, Early Years at Mount Dora Bible, New Grandma, Last Christmas, and Last Golf Tournament to see InBee Park that played on our golf team. `

When we moved to Mount Dora, Florida and Jeannie and I were teaching in the Lake Country School System for two years, then I went into business for myself, and Jeannie transferred to Mount Dora Bible (MDB), in 2016, changed the name to Mount Dora Christian Academy.

Jeannie taught there for 22 years before retiring in 2014. I started coaching the Boys Golf Team in 1991, and around 2000, I started a girls' golf team and told Jeannie she could take it over when she was ready. For the first few years, I helped her a lot, but as she got the hang of it, she became an awesome coach.

In 2002, I helped a local Korean golfer recruit some players from Korea to start a golf academy. One of the players we recruited was a young, 12-year-old, 8th grader, named InBee Park. Little did we know that she was another God send to our lives and our school. There are too many beautiful memories we shared to list them all. But you can see a few photos of her wins in the photo below. You will also see the balls from her 2002 Junior Championship, which she won, and the Golden Cased Balls from her 2016 Olympic Gold Medal in Brazil.

The personal relationship we established was a blessing to our lives, especially for Jeannie before she passed. Inbee would always send us two of everything because she knew we both loved her like our own daughter. She would send us hats from her championships, balls, personal ball markers, and signed photos from holding her tournament trophy.

When her parents were absent, Inbee would give us parent passes so we could go into the clubhouse and dine with herher awesome husband.

I thought, wow, what a God send! I recruited her to join our golf team in 2003, and we went to the High School State Golf Tournament for the first time ever; she finished 3rd at State as an 8th grader. She lived with her mom and sister, Inah, who also joined our team and played great as well.

InBee left our school after the 9th grade and moved to California to attend a golf school to advance her play. At the end of High School, she joined the LPGA and at 19 was the youngest to ever win the US Open. She went on to have a stellar career, winning 7 Major Tournaments and 31 wins overall.

This is Jeannie in January 2020. It was her last tournament to see Inbee before she passed.

2019 Last Christmas with Jeannie

I still cherish my memories of my beautiful bride, and all the time we spent on the road going to the Tampa Bay Buccaneers games together. I always liked to please her, so I was easily persuaded to drive an hour out of our way to eat at Rusty Bellies, in Tarpon Springs, before or after the game.

Losing a loved one is hard on any soulmate, but losing Jeannie's positive spirit from our family was a big loss for all of us, including many of our friends and many of her students.

She had adopted Mike Alstott, our friend and favorite Buccaneer, as her son, and loved cheering him on when we went to the games.

As I look back on our lives together, I can clearly see that God had us in His hands and was directing our steps before we ever met. He directed our steps throughout our lives through lots of challenges, followed by lots of laughter and lots of great memories. I can truly see how God used a BEAUTIFUL DAY to create a BEAUTIFUL life and write a BEAUTIFUL STORY, OUR God STORY, from its beginning to its end. God knew the stories he would create in our lives before he ever brought us together. What an awesome God! It is amazing what God knows and what we can't even imagine.

We never knew when Inbee, Inah and their mom moved to Mount Dora, Florida, that we would create a lifelong bond with an LPGA golf legend. We did not know we would be attending many LPGA events and dining with her and her family on many occasions. I did not know that Jeannie would have a surprise video from Inbee at her last birthday party.

Inbee was just another special gift that God sent our way to bring more joy to our lives. Who has God sent your way to bring added joy to your life? If the answer came quickly, then you are beginning to recognize your own God stories. So, get started, and share them.

Chapter 15

Final God Story-My Grands

November 1980

When I was a young dad, I reflected on my unstable life and made a promise to myself to do better. I committed to being a strong Christian father, determined to provide a better life for my family than the one I had experienced. I prayed for God's guidance to help me avoid falling into Satan's destructive traps. I diligently studied God's word to learn how to be a good Christian husband and father, and I attended and hosted many Bible classes on creating a Christian home.

I worked hard to apply the wisdom I gained, always striving to set a positive example for my wife and children and to all those around me.

My goal was to inspire them to follow in my footsteps. Ultimately, before my time on earth came to an end, I wanted to be able to say to both me and God:

3 John 4 (New International Version): "I have no greater joy than to hear that my children are walking in the truth."

A second secret goal I had was to live long enough to become a granddad, or "Papa," and to set a good example for my grandchildren, and including them in the verse above: "I have no greater joy than to hear that my children (and my grandchildren) are walking in the truth."

I didn't know at the time that this wish would be granted, but God did. I feel incredibly blessed to have lived a life filled with many God stories and to have a close walk with God, allowing me to see that He had great plans for me from birth through this fourth quarter of life.

One of the happiest moments of my life occurred on Christmas Day in 2024. I enjoyed brunch with my daughter, son, and two grandsons. Since my birthday is on Christmas Day, I announced to my family, "Papa is starting the first day of the fourth quarter of my life." My oldest grandson, Zane (in the above photo), quickly chimed in, "Papa, I hope you make it to overtime."

His words touched my heart, and I felt the depth of his love. It's wonderful when your children express their love for you, but hearing such profound affection and respect from my grandson made me feel special.

I did not know I would receive such a wonderful, "GRAND," Christmas blessing, but God did.

I hope my stories have served you well. May God open your eyes so you might see the glories of his mighty hands at work in your precious life. I did not know I would write this book, but God did.

Jude 1:21: "Keep yourselves in God's love as you wait for the mercy of our Lord Jesus Christ to bring you to eternal life."

3 John 1:4: "I have no greater joy than to hear that my children (and Grands) are walking in the truth."

Titus 1 (New International Version):

1: "Paul, a servant of God and an apostle of Jesus Christ to further the faith of God's elect and their knowledge of the truth that leads to godliness."

2: "In the hope of eternal life, which God, who does not lie, promised before the beginning of time,"

Jeremiah 29:11: "For I know the plans I have for you," declares the Lord, "plans to prosper you and not to harm you, plans to give you hope and a future."

Proverbs 3:5-6: "Trust in the Lord with all your heart and lean not on your own understanding; in all your ways submit to him, and he will make your paths straight."

The Armor of God

Ephesians 6:10-19:

10: "Finally, be strong in the Lord and in his mighty power."

11: "Put on the full armor of God, so that you can take your stand against the devil's schemes."

12: "For our struggle is not against flesh and blood, but against the rulers, against the authorities, against the powers of this dark world and against the spiritual forces of evil in the heavenly realms."

13: "Therefore put on the full armor of God, so that when the day of evil comes, you may be able to stand your ground, and after you have done everything, to stand."

14: "Stand firm then, with the belt of truth buckled around your waist, with the breastplate of righteousness in place,"

15: "And with your feet fitted with the readiness that comes from the gospel of peace."

16: "In addition to all this, take up the shield of faith, with which you can extinguish all the flaming arrows of the evil one."

17: "Take the helmet of salvation and the sword of the Spirit, which is the word of God."

18: "And pray in the Spirit on all occasions with all kinds of prayers and requests. With this in mind, be alert and always keep on praying for all the Lord's people."

19: "Pray also for me, that whenever I speak, words may be given me so that I will fearlessly make known the mystery of the gospel."

www.ingramcontent.com/pod-product-compliance
Lightning Source LLC
Chambersburg PA
CBHW051326120626
46547CB00015B/2408